P9-DFR-540

CREATING FANTASY ART
How To Draw
GOTHIC
FANTASY ART

STEVE BEAUMONT

Published in 2018 by
The Rosen Publishing Group, Inc.
29 East 21st Street
New York, NY 10010

Library of Congress Cataloging-in-Publication Data

Names: Beaumont, Steve, author.
Title: How to draw gothic fantasy art / Steve Beaumont.
Description: New York : Rosen Publishing, 2018. | Series: Creating fantasy art | Includes bibliographical references and index. | Audience: Grades 7–12.
Identifiers: LCCN 2017003113 | ISBN 9781499466713 (library-bound) | ISBN 9781499466744 (pbk.) | ISBN 9781538380031 (6-pack)
Subjects: LCSH: Fantasy in art—Juvenile literature. | Drawing—Technique—Juvenile literature.
Classification: LCC NC825.F25 B425 2018 | DDC 741.2—dc23
LC record available at https://lccn.loc.gov/2017003113

Manufactured in the United States of America

Copyright © 2014 Arcturus Holdings Ltd., 2018

Credits
Thanks to the following artists' materials brands that appear in this book:
Copic® [Copic is a trademark of Too Corporation in Japan], Derwent,
Faber-Castell, Letraset, Staedtler, Winsor & Newton.

All illustrations are original. Credits for additional images: Shutterstock: 31, 42.

CONTENTS

WEREWOLF

ELF PRINCESS

GARGOYLE

INTRODUCTION

As a child, I liked nothing better than losing myself in a sci-fi or horror movie or a pile of superhero comics. My favorite films were the ones that featured creatures created by Ray Harryhausen and included *Jason and the Argonauts, One Million Years BC* and *The Golden Voyage of Sinbad,* in which, for me, the animated characters rather than the actors played the starring roles.

These stop-motion model animation (dynamation as it became known) movies had a huge impact on me, as did the work of Jack Kirby, the legendary comic book artist, and Frank Frazetta, whose work I still regard today as the best in fantasy art. Indeed, I believe that had I not been impressed by Jack Kirby's art work and wanted to copy it, I may never have picked up a pencil and started to draw.

Drawn by Steve Beaumont, aged 6.

Unfortunately my passion for fantasy art, sci-fi and comics was not shared by the teachers at my school, who considered it to be a futile pursuit.

It was my dream to go to art college and learn to draw to a professional standard, but a series of events shattered those dreams and I never did get that opportunity. However, my love of fantasy art did not die and I continued to watch fantasy movies and read superhero comics, which inspired me to create my own fantasy art. I believe art college is a good place to develop your skills as an illustrator and education is paramount, but I do not think that it is the only path to success in illustration. My own experience has shown me that determination, a love of drawing and continuous practice will get you there in the end. Indeed, the purpose of this book is to encourage others to develop their fantasy art drawing skills, whether they have been lucky enough to have had an education in art or not.

This book is an entry-level guide to fantasy art. For the most part all you will need is a decent set of pencils, an eraser and some good-quality paper, as most of the exercises in this volume were produced with exactly those materials. All the exercises can be executed with varying levels of success depending on how much work you are prepared to put in. It all comes down to practice and attention to detail, which in turn comes from being observant and willing to learn. I wasn't born being able to draw the way I can now (as you can see from my childhood drawing on page 4); my skills developed over time and required practice, imagination and a lot of resolve. I am now a freelance artist producing illustrations, concept art and storyboards for the film, television and video game industries, and I have illustrated a number of graphic novels. The tutorials in this book are based on fantasy art classes that I teach at Swarthmore Learning Center, Leeds (UK).

Although the purpose of this book is for you to have fun discovering the possibilities of fantasy art, it may also awaken talents that could lead to something more. Whatever the future holds, I hope that the book will inspire you to pick up a pencil and create some wild imaginings too.

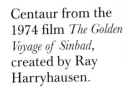

Centaur from the 1974 film *The Golden Voyage of Sinbad*, created by Ray Harryhausen.

Materials

Artists use a wide variety of materials. Some choose to work in watercolors, some prefer oils or acrylics, while others decide to use inks, pencils or pastels. I suggest that you test all these mediums because only by trying them yourself will you find the right one for you.

The items I have presented here are by no means the only brands available, but they are the ones that I use on a regular basis and, indeed, that I used to create the drawings contained within this book.

PENCILS
There is a huge range of pencils available, and it is worth trying out a few to see which you prefer.

PENCIL WEIGHTS
Here is a list of pencil weights and their qualities:
- H leads are hard and create a lighter mark on the paper. The range consists of H–9H, with 9H being the hardest.
- HB pencils are a good mid-range pencil, giving a wide variety of tone between the H and B leads.
- B leads are softer and leave a lot of lead on the paper, which is easily smudged. The range consists of B–9B, with 9B being the softest.

ERASERS
There are lots of erasers on the market, but only a select few good products. I tend to use Winsor & Newton putty rubbers (Figure 1), Staedtler plastic erasers (Figure 2), and a Derwent battery-operated eraser (Figure 3).

Figure 2

Figure 1

Figure 3

BLENDERS
A lot of pencil work involves blending pencil lead to give a smooth area of tone or to create clouds of smoke or other effects. To create these I use tissue paper wrapped around my index finger or a blending stump (Figure 4).

PAPER
Most of the drawings in this book were produced on 180gsm acid-free cartridge paper. Generally, choose a good-quality cartridge paper of a reasonably sturdy weight, as this will prevent your artwork from easily being creased and bent. There are many brands of paper on the market, including Winsor & Newton, Derwent, Daler, Canson and Snowdon, all of which produce good-quality cartridge paper as well as lower-quality student pads for practicing on.

Figure 4

INKING

Inking requires a lot more concentration than mark-making with a pencil, as every pen/brush stroke is permanent.

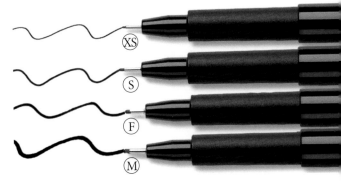

INK PENS

Faber-Castell Pitt Artist pens and Copic Multiliners are the brands I tend to use for inking and, although I do try out other brands and experiment with other tools, these are the pens that I feel most comfortable working with. They were also used to create the inked drawings in this book.

Figure 5

WATERCOLOR BRUSHES

Watercolor brushes (Figure 5) are also great for inking, although inking with a brush is not as easy as using a pen and takes a lot more practice. The beauty of using brushes for inking, however, is that they come in a wide variety of sizes and, in the case of the much larger brushes, enable you to quickly cover larger areas with black.

MARKER PENS

I use marker pens for quite a lot of my coloring as the hues are vibrant and can be manipulated by using a blender fluid. There are a number of brands of marker pen available, but by far the most popular are the Letraset Tria and the Copic Marker.

Three-Nib Pen by Letraset

Two-nib pen by Copic

Figure Drawing

The job of a fantasy artist is to make the unreal seem real and the unbelievable, believable. Almost all fantasy art contains human or human-like figures, whether these are 'normal' or distorted beings or some kind of creature that walks on two legs. They can all be drawn with more conviction if the artist is familiar with basic anatomy.

BASIC ANATOMY

A study of the human skeleton is essential, but it is not necessary to know the names of every single bone. Nor do you have to draw a full skeleton every time you sketch a figure; by studying the structure you can simplify it and break it down into some basic shapes. The key is to get the proportions correct.

The image on the left (Figure 1) shows a human skeleton, and the image on the right (Figure 2) shows how this can be broken down into a more manageable frame, which can then be used as the basis of a figure. At this stage, the limbs can be represented by simple stick lines and the rib cage and hips as basic oval shapes.

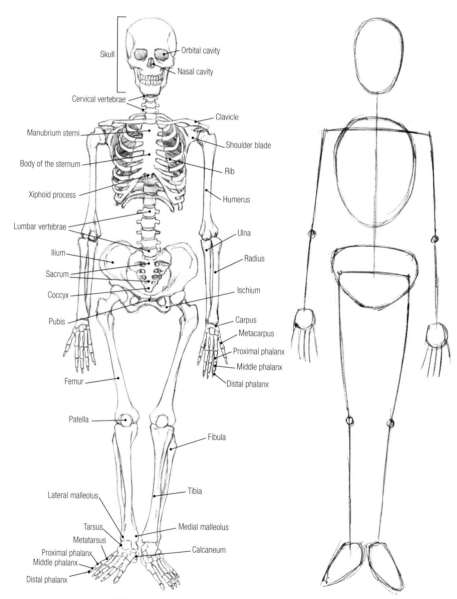

Figure 1   **Figure 2**

FIGURES IN ACTION

Once you are familiar with the skeleton, try drawing some rough sketches of stick figures in action. If you are drawing someone throwing a punch or swinging a sword, try to imagine the action and the direction of movement, and where the body weight is distributed. For instance, if the figure is throwing a punch it is more than likely that all the body weight will be supported by the leg that is farthest forward rather than by the rear leg.

You also need to consider the flow of movement and action. This flow can be simplified by a single stroke of a pen. This is evident when you look at the images of the upright figure with the staff in its left hand (below); one is annotated with arrows that indicate the direction of the twists and bends of the body, while in the alternative image the line of the pose has been simplified to a brush stroke.

DRAWING THE HEAD

Learning to draw a human head is critical as most pieces of fantasy art contain a human figure or a variation of one. The proportions of a human skull will usually fit within a square. By dividing this square into four equal sections you can determine the position of the eye line (which is situated about halfway between the top of the head and the chin) and the center line (the vertical mid-line). These two lines will help you to correctly place the features of the face. Figure 1 shows the head in profile. Note that the end of the nose sits roughly halfway between the center line/eyes and the chin, and the top of the visible ear is aligned with the eye. Figure 2 shows you how to plot the face when viewing it from the front. When drawing the eyes, divide the head across its width into five equal spaces. The eyes will sit in the second and fourth spaces. Of course, in reality the human face varies tremendously and can be many shapes and sizes, but applying these guidelines to whatever shape head you are drawing should help you create a balanced face.

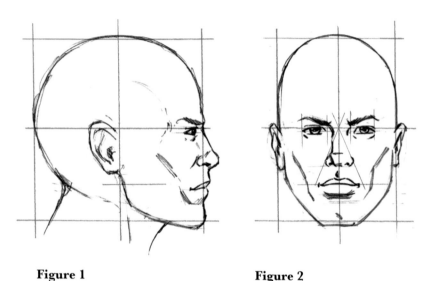

Figure 1   **Figure 2**

Another popular technique for drawing a head is to use a ball and a cube shape. Figure 3 shows the head constructed around these forms. The same principle can be applied whatever the angle of the head, whether shown at a three-quarter view (Figure 4) or a lowered three-quarter view (Figure 5).

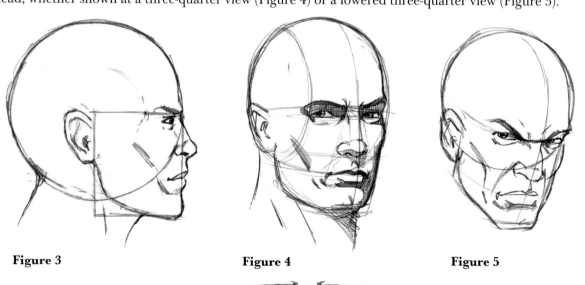

Figure 3   **Figure 4**   **Figure 5**

Here we have the female face. Figure 6 shows a round, young-looking face, while in Figure 7 you can see that by using a narrower grid to produce a thinner face the figure appears slightly older. Notice the shape of the eyes, which are larger and rounder (although essentially still oval) than those of a male, and the shape and thickness of the eyebrows. Using slightly bigger eyes on a female character will often make her appear more attractive. Also notice the shape of the female chin in Figure 8, which is narrower and more refined than that of a male, who would be likely to have a square jaw and flatter chin.

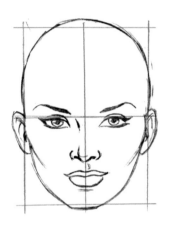

Figure 6

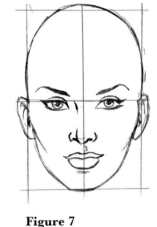

Figure 7

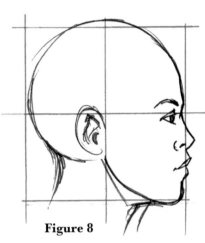

Figure 8

As with the male head, I have simplified the construction of the face and head to a ball and a cube shape (Figure 9). Have fun drawing the head at different angles (Figures 10–12). It may help to study your own head in the mirror at different angles, noticing what is visible and what is not when the head is tilted back, or turned three-quarters to the left or right, or tilted down slightly. You can learn a lot from studying your own face in the mirror, especially when trying to capture expressions.

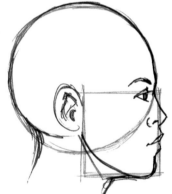

Figure 9

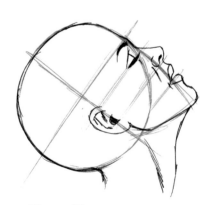

Figure 10

Figure 11

Figure 12

COLORING

For the best part of my career I have been a traditional artist. By "traditional" I mean that I usually work with pencils, inks and paint on paper, board or canvas rather than creating images digitally. About 70 percent of my concept art and storyboard work is colored using Copic markers and sometimes colored pencils, but more recently I have begun coloring my work using Photoshop. This change came about by chance, when I placed an order for some materials but only a few were immediately available: the other items arrived later but not in time for me to meet a work deadline, so I decided to color the piece digitally. At the time I used a mouse, which was a slow and clumsy device for certain parts of the coloring. However, the final piece pleased the client so much that I invested in a Wacom graphics tablet. I have since discovered that working with a tablet enables me to work more quickly and saves a lot of money that I would normally spend on materials. I still consider myself a traditional artist, but today more often I merge traditional and digital techniques, gaining the best of both worlds as they each offer different benefits.

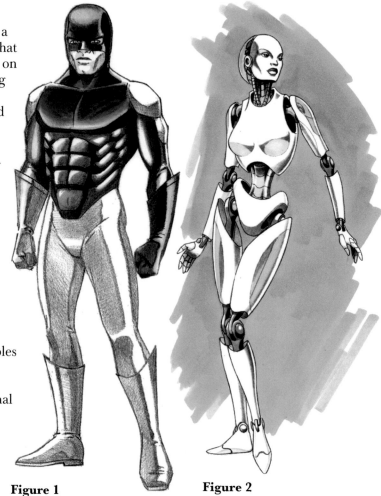

Figure 1

Figure 2

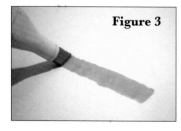

Figure 3

Figure 4

I approach coloring my work digitally in the same way as I would if I were using markers or watercolors and, to some extent, acrylic or oils. I apply a pale wash as a background for the rest of the colors to sit on, which adds depth. I build up the colors using layers, all set to Multiply. This allows colors to interact and blend with the layers. If I were working on a pure white background I could end up with bits of white showing through where the brush strokes are lighter or broken, which

would create a brighter, breezier image. This could be fine if that is the effect you want to achieve. Figure 1 and Figure 2 are examples of traditional concept art, colored using Copic markers. I started by laying down a single flat coat of ink with the pen (Figure 3). Figure 4 demonstrates how I built up the depth of color by applying more layers of the same shade. You should be able to see the strength variations as the layers cross over one another.

COLORING WITH MARKERS VS DIGITAL COLORING

Figures 5–10 demonstrate how markers and digital coloring work in pretty much the same way. The images in the left-hand column were created using Copic markers on paper and the images in the right-hand column were created digitally.

If you closely examine the lines created by the marker, you will see that the ink creates a texture as it soaks into the fibers of the paper. This can lend a pleasing quality to illustrations and concept art in the same way that the random and uneven drying of ink or watercolor washes can. Digital coloring always tends to be cleaner and brighter than manual coloring, which can be desirable. Both methods have their own unique benefits that will enhance your art and I will be using both in this book.

COLORING AN IMAGE USING PHOTOSHOP

Although I do not give explicit instructions regarding coloring images using Photoshop, or the exact CMYK colors I used, it is helpful to have a rough idea of how to start experimenting with this program. The best way to learn is simply to give things a go; that is the main benefit of digital images – unlike hard-copy drawings they can be replicated and saved as separate files so you can try out infinite variations.

1. Scan the finished drawing and save it as a tiff or psd file. Import this file into Photoshop.

2. Create a new layer (Layer 1), then choose the Fill option and select a shade for the base layer. Adjust the opacity until you are happy with the result. Choose the Multiply option from the drop-down menu, which will ensure the layer is transparent.

3. Add details to specific areas of the picture using one of the many brushes and the palette of colors available. It is a good idea to create a new layer, set to Multiply,

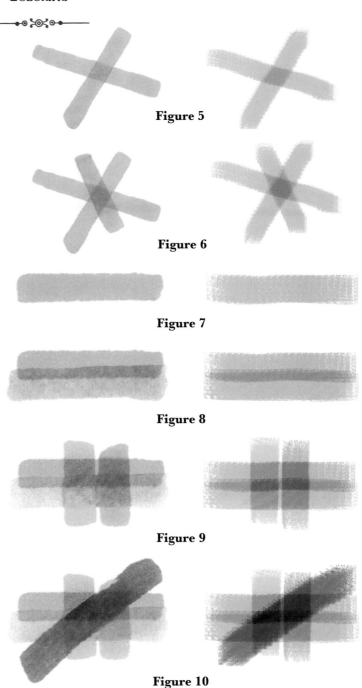

Figure 5

Figure 6

Figure 7

Figure 8

Figure 9

Figure 10

for each level of detailing so that you can amend them individually. There are many brushes available online, but I sometimes create my own by scanning ink spatters, pencil rubbings and cross-hatching I have produced on paper.

4. To add highlights, use a brush tool set to Normal rather than Multiply, since you don't want highlights to be transparent or to blend with the layers underneath.

WEREWOLF

The werewolf reminds us of primal instincts within us all. It is a classic subject for lovers of horror films and fantasy art and really good fun to draw. I am a big fan of the 1941 Universal Pictures horror movie *The Wolf Man*, starring Lon Chaney, Jr. in the title role. This picture demonstrates how effective a simple layout and the application of color and lighting with just a handful of markers can be.

I started by sketching a few scenarios in order to work out the setting and stance of the character. My first idea was to have the werewolf howling on a clifftop above a small village (Figure 1), to imply that this was where the beast would find its next victims. However, much as I liked this idea, I felt that there wasn't sufficient focus on the beast itself, so I tried another approach and came up with Figure 2. This way, by making the werewolf larger, I could include more detail (Figure 3).

Figure 1

Figure 2

Figure 3

STEP 4

Once you have drawn the head, face and hands and are satisfied with them, add the clothing. I have purposely made it so torn and tattered that it is impossible to get an impression of period. The position of the light source, the full moon, creates heavy shadows which also contribute to the vagueness of the clothing's appearance.

STEP 5

Trace the working drawing on to a piece of pale blue A3 paper using a lightbox. If you do not have a lightbox, you can do an image transfer instead. Rub a soft lead pencil across the back of the working drawing, completely covering the piece of paper. Tape the drawing to the A3 paper so that the covered side is securely positioned face down on the clean sheet and the working drawing is face up. Firmly trace over the working drawing with a biro or hard lead pencil. This will transfer the lead pencil on the underside of the drawing on to the clean sheet as an outline. Whichever method you use, you are aiming to create a clean outline on the blue piece of paper (Figure 11).

Figure 11

STEP 6

Using a Copic Multiliner brush pen, begin inking the drawing. This is a very easy inking job as it is mostly solid. Try to use the versatility of the brush nib to create a variety of line thicknesses so that the drawing does not look too technical and rigid.

Here you can see the final inked drawing. If you had drawn this on white paper, you would have an exciting black-and-white drawing of a werewolf. But since this piece has been created on colored paper, you can create more atmosphere using five Copic markers and a Pentel correction pen, as I will show you in the next few pages.

STEP 7
Use an Ice Blue (Copic B12) marker to create the base layer for the clouds and grass. I also used this marker to make a base layer for the darker tones of color on the clothing and fur.

STEP 8

Create the darker tones of the sky with a Phthalo Blue (Copic B23) marker. This is not a particularly dark marker but, layered over the Ice Blue, it creates the right shade. I also applied it to the grass, clothing and hair to build up the color tones. Apply Warm Grey 2 (Copic WG2) to the fur and clothing, leaving highlights on the areas nearest the source of light (the moon). Warm greys are very useful for building up tone and texture.

STEP 9

Apply Warm Grey 5 (Copic WG5) to blend the lighter tones and the solid blacks, particularly in the creases of the clothes and the areas of the fur nearest the solid black. Use a Pentel correction pen to create white highlights round the outline of the figure and on random blades of grass. White gouache or Permanent White and a fine brush would create the same effect.

STEP 10

Use a white crayon pencil to add soft detail to the moon.

STEP 11

For the final touch, use a vermillion red (Copic R08) marker to draw the blood on the mouth, hand and clothing. Once layered over the darker tones, the red ink creates a blood-like effect.

Elf Príncess

This exercise is a good way to build up your confidence in figure drawing before tackling more complex characters. The main point of focus here is achieving the correct stance, as the attitude of the figure is conveyed through the pose. Drawing the character will also give you a chance to tackle clothing, armor and accessories, all of which are part of character design.

STEP 1

Begin by drawing a skeleton frame, using the techniques outlined on pages 16–17 and referring to this image as a guide. It is important to get the stance right before moving on to the next stage. If the pose is not balanced, all the shading and armor in the world will not disguise the fact that the figure's pose is weak.

STEP 2

Once the skeletal figure has been drawn with the correct stance, flesh out the outer shape of the body and check the stance again, as it is easy to start over at this stage if you find it is unbalanced. The red arrows in Figure 1 clearly show the various angles of the pose. Notice that the figure is putting her body weight on her right leg (her left as we are looking at her), which is causing her hip to tilt and her left leg to bend. Her shoulders are also affected by the position of her legs – her right shoulder is lower than her left. The angle of the head is also important – notice that it turns towards us, adding another twist to the spine.

Figure 1

STEP 3

Once the pose has been established and you are happy with the balance of it, the rest of the body can be fleshed out. The breasts rest on the ribcage area and for now can be round or slightly oval. When drawing the face, keep the features simple. Try not to overwork it by adding too many lines. Notice I have not drawn the entire line for the nose, merely implying its position by carefully placing nostrils in the correct place. Because the head is tilting downwards, her eyes are looking slightly up through her eyebrows (Figures 2 and 3). Once you are happy with the face, you can carefully erase the guidelines (Figure 4).

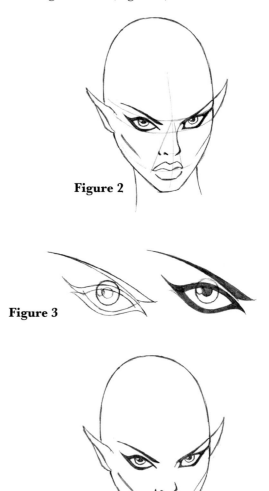

Figure 2

Figure 3

Figure 4

STEP 4

Now you can add details such as
the hair and cape. Keep the shapes
simple when drawing the hair. Go
for curves that are aesthetically
pleasing and try not to make things
unnecessarily complicated. The
same applies to the cape that hangs
from her shoulders. When it comes
to drawing clothing, a good point of
reference is to look in the mirror and
observe how garments fit and hang
from your own body. For the cape,
you could throw a sheet or blanket
over your shoulders to see how it
hangs down.

STEP 5

The clothing worn by the character now needs to be drawn. I chose a leather or rubber bodysuit that adhered to the contours of the body, and added belts, straps and chains to lend the figure extra interest. I also gave her a pair of metallic gauntlets, which make her hands appear more powerful.

This part of the design process is where the character develops, so it is important to think about what details to add and where to position them. You can gain inspiration for different looks in many places, from the high street and fashion shows to books, magazines, movies, video games or the Internet. For this character I referenced photographs of medieval armor. When drawing the chains, think about the thickness of each link and how they interlock with each other (Figure 5), and try to render this accurately.

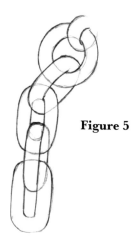

Figure 5

STEP 6

Having established the main shapes and position of the clothing and any embellishments, these can now be decorated with finer detail. When it came to drawing the detail on the gauntlet (Figure 6), I took inspiration from a book on medieval armor (Figure 7). It is essential to have a point of reference when drawing an unusual item, if you hope to represent it correctly. Before applying the first layers of shading, I decided to alter the clasp for the cape. I felt the original shape was a bit boring, so I changed it to a more interesting demonic skull shape (Figure 8).

Figure 6

Figure 7

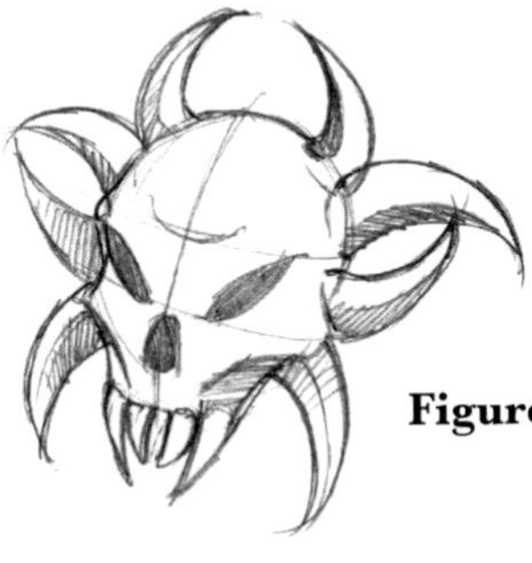

Figure 8

STEP 7

Once the outline drawing has been finished, areas of tone need to be blocked in. I applied an even layer of shading for the base layer. As I knew there were not going to be too many layers of tone for her clothing, I applied an overall dark tone using a B lead. Leave areas of white for the highlights on the left-hand side (as we are looking at the picture), which indicate that the main light source is to the left of the picture. This will make it easier to strengthen the highlights with an eraser later. As this drawing is not a full figure and does not include the lower legs and feet, the shading gradually fades out at the bottom of the page.

STEP 8

Once you are happy with the base layer, softly blend it with tissue paper, then apply a second layer for the darker tones on her hair (Figure 9), the underside of her breasts and the inside and folds of her cape. For blending the hair I used a No. 5 blending stump (Figure 10).

Figure 9

Figure 10

STEP 9

Once the blending is correct, apply highlights with an eraser. Use the fine edge of a plastic eraser or mould a putty rubber into a fine point to get into the more fiddly details, such as the belts and chains (Figure 11). Define the highlights by chiselling away with the sharp edge of an eraser. Think of the eraser as adding and not removing – rather as if you were painting white highlights with permanent white gouache. The light source is mostly coming from the left of the figure as we are looking at her, so the bolder highlights are on the left-hand side, with some less dominant ones to the right, indicating a weaker light source to the right.

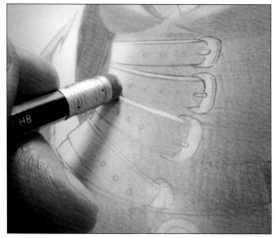

Figure 11

Having applied all the final shading and highlighting, clean up around the outside of the drawing with an eraser, being careful not to erase any of your drawing (Figure 12).

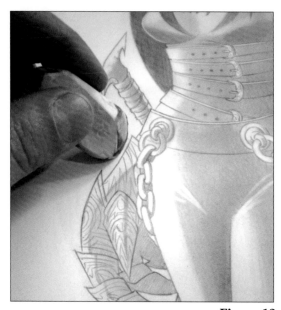

Figure 12

Finally, go around the drawing using a sharp HB pencil and add a crisp, hard line to any areas that need defining (Figure 13), such as the outline of the hair and cape and the detail of the gauntlet and belt. The finished drawing can be seen on the facing page.

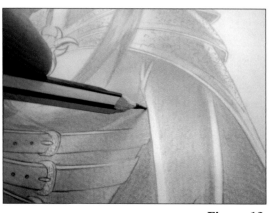

Figure 13

GARGOYLE

This last exercise is typical of a quick sketch session, during which I take a class through a sketch from beginning to end in one and a half hours. The purpose of the exercise is to show how easily and effectively a drawing can be achieved in a short space of time. Often these are produced on colored paper and inked with a Faber-Castell Pitt Artist pen and a colored marker that complements the choice of paper.

Figure 1

Figure 2

Figure 3

Figure 4

Figure 5

Figure 6

The materials you will need for this exercise are: grey or stone colored paper (Figure 1); permanent white gouache (Figure 2); No. 0 or No. 2 watercolor brush (Figure 3) or a Pentel correction pen (Figure 4); Faber-Castell Pitt Artist pen (Figure 5); B26 Cobalt Blue or a B29 Ultramarine Copic marker (Figure 6).

To get a feel for the look of the gargoyle, source some photo reference, as shown in Figure 7 and Figure 8. On my travels, I often take photographs of any architecture that I think is interesting or that will possibly come in useful for reference on a future project. For this drawing, I used photographs of St Martin's Church on Coney Street in York (England) (Figure 9 and Figure 10).

Figure 7

Figure 8

Figure 9

Figure 10

PERSPECTIVE

The main things to consider when working from a photograph are the angles and perspectives inherent in the shot. Some settings can provide striking backdrops for additional imagery that you may wish to superimpose. In this exercise, the Gothic building and upward-looking perspective lend themselves well to a winged figure, and a gargoyle seemed an apt subject.

In order to draw both the setting and the gargoyle correctly you will require some knowledge of perspective drawing, so the aim of this section is to outline the basic rules. Figure 11 shows a railway track disappearing into the distance. Notice how the rails get closer together the further away they are from the foreground. The point at which they meet is called a point of perspective or a vanishing point. The horizontal line that crosses the point of perspective is called the horizon line.

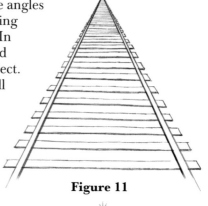

Figure 11

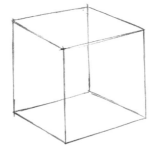

Figure 12

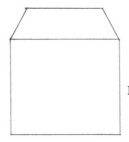

Figure 13

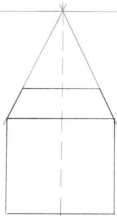

Figure 14

We shall use a basic cube (Figure 12) to show how the rules of perspective work. If we turn the cube so we are looking at it straight on (Figure 13) you will notice that the two sides on the top of the cube appear to draw closer together, or converge, towards the back. If these lines are extended, they will eventually meet (Figure 14). The point at which they meet determines the horizon line. This is called single or one-point perspective because the perspective lines meet at a single point.

When the cube is turned so that the corner point faces the front (Figure 15), we get two-point perspective below the horizon line (eye level). If the viewpoint changes, so does the horizon line (Figure 16).

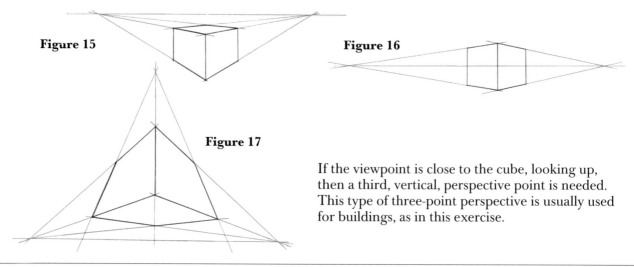

Figure 15

Figure 16

Figure 17

If the viewpoint is close to the cube, looking up, then a third, vertical, perspective point is needed. This type of three-point perspective is usually used for buildings, as in this exercise.

A

STEP 1

Start by plotting the layout. I have used white paper for this exercise to make the steps clearer, but you can draw directly on to colored paper. The vanishing points for this drawing go right off the page, so roughly gauge the perspective or (loosely) tape extra paper to the main sheet and work out your vanishing points in full.

Draw a vanishing point above the figure and converge the lines that demarcate the outline of the figure at that point (A). You can then gauge the angle of the castellations on the top of the wall, drawing diagonal downward lines from left to right (B) towards an imagined vanishing point off the paper. To create a three-dimensional effect and give the castellations depth you need to add a further set of diagonal lines travelling in the opposite direction (C) towards another imagined vanishing point off the paper, creating three-point perspective. Figure 18 is a cleaned-up version so that you can see how the different components in the image work once they have been correctly positioned.

B

C

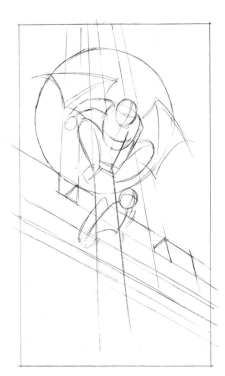

Figure 18

STEP 2

Once you have plotted the layout and are happy with the perspective, apply some detail to the architecture, defining the stonework and the gargoyle. Note the use of the full moon, which will create a framing device for the gargoyle.

STEP 3
Develop the detail of
the gargoyle's character,
taking pointers from the
photo references you
have collated. The face
here is almost like that
of a small dragon.

STEP 4
Shading can now be applied to the
areas that will be mostly solid black.
In reality, if a full moon this size were
directly behind the gargoyle you
would mostly see a silhouette, so to
make the drawing more interesting
I have used some artistic licence and
inserted some additional off-frame
light sources.

STEP 5

Once all the pencil work is complete, apply the ink. I used a brush pen for this drawing as it enabled me to create some bold line work as well as enabling me to pick out delicate lines from the stonework details. First, I went over all the line work with ink, then I filled in the solid areas. I purposely created an uneven line with the pen to give the impression of old, worn and weathered stone (Figure 19). The brush pen is perfect for this kind of line work.

Figure 19

STEP 6

Once the inking is completed it is time to add color. I used a B26 (Cobalt Blue) Copic marker to color the sky. When attempting to color a large area with a marker, always study the drawing first and decide the best position to begin from. Never start in the middle of an area or in a place that will lead you in two different directions. The important thing to remember is to keep the ink flowing until you have covered the required area. I started at the left-hand side of the drawing as it allowed me to put down a continuous flow of ink all the way round to the other side.

STEP 7

The gargoyle is looking a bit flat against the moon, so use a white pencil (I used a chinagraph pencil, Figure 20), chalk pastel or permanent white gouache to add some detail to the moon. Use a photo (Figure 21) to help you re-create a realistic texture. This will give a sense of depth between the moon and the gargoyle.

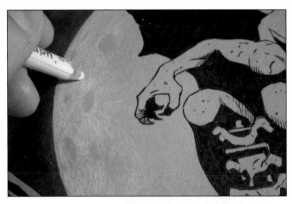

Figure 20

Figure 21

STEP 8

The moon in the background would cast light on the form of the gargoyle. To create these highlights, apply a thin line of gouache to the wings and outer areas of the creature using a No. 2 sable brush.

STEP 9

Finally, add the rain using a Pentel correction pen, which gives a solid white line with one stroke. Alternatively, try gouache and a brush, but I would advise you to practice this technique on some scrap paper before applying it to your final piece of artwork.

SKETCHBOOK

I often stress the importance of keeping sketchbooks to my students. They can be used for any kind of drawing – from observational sketches or the exploration of ideas to testing out new materials (pens, pencils, paints, etc.) or just doodling for the fun of it. All these activities help to develop drawing skills and, as with most things, the more you practice, the better you become. Professional artists fill dozens of sketchbooks. The rough workings of some, including Frank Frazetta, Jeffrey Jones and Claire Wendling, have been turned into high-end art books that showcase their creative processes. The seeds of some of your best ideas may be doodled in a sketchbook. Ideas flow uninhibited when you are not feeling too precious about your drawing and you may often experience a breakthrough in this way.

For a recent project for drawing a dragon I had so many ideas fighting to get out that I had to spend a bit of time rough-sketching all kinds of dragons and layouts in order to unclutter my head. It was also fun just to play around with shapes and capture movement, and it reminded me how enjoyable sketching can be. When I came to break down the exercise, however, I realized that such a detailed design would require too much space, so I opted for a simpler, more conventional design.

I hope you have learned something
from these exercises and that you have
developed and taken your drawing
skills to the next level, and had some
fun at the same time. The important
thing to remember is that improving
your drawing skills will not happen
overnight – it will take lots of practice.
The more you practice, the more
skilled you will become.

GLOSSARY

adhere Stick completely to something.

aesthetically pleasing Something that looks good, or attractive to the eye.

anatomy The body structure of humans and animals.

distorted Pulled and twisted out of shape.

gauntlets Long gloves that are loose around the wrists and forearms.

gouache Paint with a glue-like texture.

lightbox A flat box with a translucent top and light inside, used by artists to help when tracing pictures.

protuberance Something that juts or stands out from the surface.

sci-fi Short for science fiction.

spine Backbone.

stance The way that a person stands.

stop-motion A type of animation created using a camera that is continually stopped and started again.

superimpose To lay one thing over another.

FURTHER INFORMATION

Chris Riddell's Doodle-a-Day by Chris Riddell (Macmillan Children's Books, 2015)

Draw and Write Your Own Comics by Louie Stowell (Usborne Publishing, 2014)

Drawing Fantasy Creatures by Aaron Sautter (Capstone Press, 2016)

Drawing Manga: Step-by-Step by Ben Krefta (Arcturus Publishing, 2013)

Drawing Wizards, Witches and Warlocks by Christ Hart (Sixth and Spring Books, 2009)

How to Draw Fantasy Art by Mark Bergin (PowerKids Press, 2011)

Terry Pratchett's Discworld Colouring Book by Paul Kidby (Gollancz, 2016)

INDEX